Come, Follow Me

A Child's Guide to Faithful Choices

This book belongs to _____

Pflaum Publishing Group
Dayton, OH
Milwaukee, WI

A note to parents and catechists

Faith is a wonderful gift to share with the children in our care. We bring them to Mass, and we teach them in class, because we want faith to guide their daily decisions. We hope they will make faithful choices.

This book introduces your child to some basic concepts of faith and self-awareness. But real lessons come from real life. Model the values you want them to learn. Discuss the choices they make. Let them experience the results. Extend forgiveness and unconditional love. These lessons will tend the soil of moral integrity. You can count on that!

Text and activities by Jean Buell

First and foremost, Jean is a parent who wants her home to be a place of faith, hope, and love. In addition to parenting and writing, Jean facilitates worship and learning experiences for children and families in her home state of Minnesota. Other titles in this popular series for children include books on the Mass, Bible, saints, rosary, and sacraments. Available from Pflaum Publishing Group.

Cover illustrations by Elizabeth Swisher
Interior design by Jean Buell and Ellen Wright
Edited by Jean Larkin

Scripture references are taken from or paraphrased from the *Contemporary English Version* translation of the Bible, © American Bible Society, 1995, 1999. Used with permission.

Nihil obstat: Reverend Thomas Knoebel, February 11, 2008
Imprimatur: †Most Reverend Timothy M. Dolan, Archbishop of Milwaukee, February 26, 2008

Second Printing April 2009

Pflaum Publishing Group
2621 Dryden Road, Suite 300
Dayton, OH 45439
800-543-4383
pflaum.com

ISBN 978-1-933178-82-0

Come, Follow Me

Welcome!

How high can you count? 10? 100? 1000? You are learning to work with numbers. You are also learning to make choices—every single day!

Count your choices. What was the first choice you made today? Perhaps you chose what to wear. Or what to eat. Or what to do. Describe your choice here.

_____

_____

How many other choices did you make today? How many choices will you make in your lifetime? It will be a lot! Can you even count that high?

Your choices count! They show who you are. They show what is important to you. And they affect other people, too. Some choices are easy. Some are more difficult. Making choices is a BIG responsibility.

Count on Jesus to help. He said,

> If you keep on obeying what I have said, you truly are my disciples. You will know the truth, and the truth will set you free.
>
> (John 8:31-32)

Jesus helps us make faithful choices. He tells us about the things of God. He shows us how to act rightly. And he loves us, too! He wants us to follow him.

Can we count you in??? Turn the page!

Come,

There is...**One Incredible You**

By turning the page, you made a faithful choice to follow Jesus. The first step is to let him love you. This story shows you that Jesus already loves you!

One day, some people brought their children to Jesus for his blessing. The disciples scolded the people for bothering Jesus. But Jesus said,

> Let the children come to me! Don't try to stop them. People who are like these little children belong to the kingdom of God.

Imagine you are in the story.
Jesus holds you. Jesus blesses you.
Jesus says your name.

"_____"

Write your name here.

Jesus loves all children. He even talks about their goodness! Each person is created with goodness inside. That includes you! God is so incredibly good and full of love. When God breathed life and love into you, you became incredible too! You have goodness just because God loves you. And you have goodness just because you are you!

Your goodness includes your special personality, your special strengths, and your special skills. All these add up to **One Incredible You!**

4

Follow Me

Remember your goodness. Always. This will help you make faithful choices. If you forget your goodness, go back to this story and your imagination. Jesus loves you. Always!

**Draw yourself in this figure. Write or draw
your favorite activities, too. Look! You are incredible!**

Come,

Here are... Two Greatest Commandments

(See Mark 12:28-31.)

Many people listened to Jesus. One day, he was talking with some teachers. One teacher asked Jesus, "What is the most important commandment?" Jesus answered,

The most important commandment is: "You must love God with all your heart, soul, mind, and strength." The second most important commandment is: "Love others as much as you love yourself."

These two commandments are called the Greatest Commandments. The commandments are God's plan for how we can live our lives with love—toward God, others, and ourselves.

Some people think of the commandments as rules. Families have rules. Schools have rules. Games have rules. Rules can be helpful, and it is important to follow helpful rules.

But a commandment is even more important than a rule. It is more than helpful. It is a statement about our closeness to God and God's closeness to us.

The first of these two Greatest Commandments is about loving God above all other things. The second is about how we can bring more and more love into the world through ourselves and others. When we choose to follow these commandments, we make choices that are faithful to God's plan for us.

Count on God's goodness inside you. Now count on Jesus to guide you. That is how faithful choices begin!

Follow Me

Jesus followed the Greatest Commandments. He loved God, and he loved people. Crosses remind us of his great love. Where is a cross in your church? Your home? How can a cross remind you to follow the Greatest Commandments?

Begin at Start 1. *Follow the arrows. Copy the letters on the lines below. For each "X," leave a space. When the arrows stop, begin again with* **Start 2** *and do the same thing.*

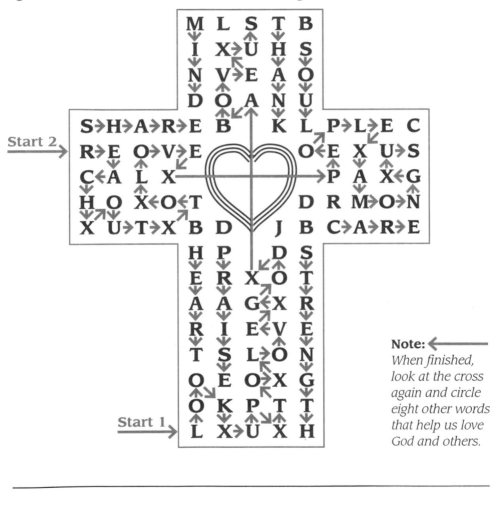

Note:
When finished, look at the cross again and circle eight other words that help us love God and others.

_____

_____

_____

Come,

Here are...Three Ways to Love One Another

(See Luke 6:27-36.)

Jesus brought lots of love to the world. He showed great love with his actions and his words. He encouraged the people to love generously, because that is how God loves.

One day, Jesus told the people to love one another, even when it is difficult. He told them to love their enemies. He said to be good to them and ask God to bless them. He told them:

Treat others just as you want to be treated.

This is called the "Golden Rule." It's easy to remember. Read it again. Now, close your eyes and say it out loud. Keep practicing until you know it by heart.

The Golden Rule is a helpful rule. It helps us stop and think. It helps us be honest with ourselves. And it helps us love one another. There are three ways to do this—

Thoughts ● Words ● Actions.

Start with this question: *How do I want other people to treat me?*
The answers will tell you what to do.

Sometimes it's easy. Sometimes it's difficult. Just do your best. Trust yourself to make faithful choices. Trust Jesus to help you bring more love into the world.

**Follow the Golden Rule.
Keep practicing till you know it!**

Follow Me

How do you want others to treat you in their thoughts? With respect, of course! Now you know how to treat others

Think Respectful Thoughts

Here's a message to find...and keep in mind! *Name each picture out loud. Listen well. Write the real words below the picture.*

God

 + d

 – b

_____

e + + e

d +  – gl

_____

L + [hook picture]

d + [clown picture] – cl

[swan picture] – sw

_____

N + E + 1

L + [hook picture]

4

_____

g + [hood picture] + [mum picture] – t

 – p

F + [tree picture] – t + **1**

_____

9

Come,

How do you want others to treat you with their words? With good manners, of course! Now you know how to treat others.

Say Polite Words

Some words are not quite polite. *Unscramble these to make them right. Then be polite each day and night!*

1. When you ask for something, say **speale** _____.

When you receive it, say **hatnk uoy** _____ _____.

2. When you meet someone, smile and say **loleh** _____.

When you leave, say **odgo yeb** _____ _____.

3. When you must interrupt, say **scuxee em** _____

_____.

4. When someone offers to give you something,

if you want it, say **eys splaee** _____ _____.

if you don't want it, say **on nathk oyu** ____ _____

_____.

5. If someone teases or tickles too much, say **POTS** _____!

If that doesn't work, yell **ELPH** _____!

Then tell an adult what happened.

Follow Me

How do you want others to treat you with their actions? With kindness, of course! Now you know how to treat others.

Act with Kindness

Got a minute? Put kindness in it! *Watch for "times" like these. Be quick to respond. The prize is joy, and you can win it!*

A kindergartner is crying because the bus seats look full. What can you do?

_____

Your classmate's pencil broke. You have two pencils. What can you do?

_____

_____

There is a meal wrapper crumpled on the ground. What can you do?

_____

_____

Your parent comes home with many bags of groceries. What can you do?

_____

_____

A new student is sitting all alone during lunch. What can you do?

_____

_____

Your pet's water dish is empty. What can you do?

_____

_____

Treat others as you want them to treat you. And treat yourself that way, too!

Come,

Here are...**Four Ways to Speak Up**

(See Luke 6:43-45.)

Jesus used examples to explain what he taught. One example was a tree and its fruit. He said,

> A good tree cannot produce bad fruit, and a bad tree cannot produce good fruit. You can tell what a tree is like by the fruit it produces. Good people do good things because of the good in their hearts. Your words show what is in your heart.

What's in our hearts? God's goodness, of course. What else? Plenty! Our hearts are full of emotions. Our minds are full of thoughts. And our bodies are full of sensations. There is a lot going on inside!

Words are important. They help us name what is going on— inside and outside. They help us ask for what we want and need. And they help us ask for help! That is what it means to speak up. Count on people you trust to listen to you—parents, teachers, family, and friends.

When we don't speak up, our thoughts and feelings get all mixed up. We get stuck. And we forget God's goodness inside. Then it becomes more difficult to make faithful choices.

Here are some helpful words to start your sentences when you speak up.

- **I think**...
- **I feel**...
- **I need**...
- **I want**...

Follow Me

Do say **I think** to talk about ideas and opinions. Be respectful. Choose polite words.

Do say **I feel** to talk about emotions. Choose words like happy, sad, angry, or afraid. Don't say, *"It doesn't matter,"* because it does!

Look for emotions in this puzzle. Look for them in your daily life, too. Then use these words to speak up!

```
E  C  O  N  F  I  D  E  N  T  Y  G
T  M  E  X  C  I  T  E  D  X  L  L
H  J  B  Z  G  R  U  M  P  Y  L  A
A  F  R  A  I  D  M  S  O  U  I  D
N  A  N  G  R  Y  B  H  F  S  S  J
K  P  B  H  U  R  T  Y  J  A  B  E
F  R  U  S  T  R  A  T  E  D  O  A
U  L  O  N  E  L  Y  S  J  M  R  L
L  H  A  P  P  Y  K  M  S  B  E  O
J  E  S  U  R  P  R  I  S  E  D  U
M  B  D  E  S  U  F  N  O  C  D  S
```

Word List

afraid	embarrassed	happy	sad
angry	excited	hurt	shy
bored	frustrated	jealous	silly
confident	glad	lonely	surprised
confused	grumpy	playful	thankful

Come,

Do say **I need** to talk about things that help you survive, like food and water. These things are basic. Pets need them, too. Also say *Please* and *Thank you*. (Don't say *Arf!* or *Meow!*)

Do say **I want** to talk about your wishes. Some are practical and some are playful. Also say *Please* and *Thank you*. Don't say *Gimme this!* or *Gimme that!*

What's the difference between **needs** and **wants**? *Use two colors of crayons or highlighters. Lightly fill the squares in a checkerboard pattern. Then read the words of each color. One color will be needs; the other will be wants.*

air	candy	water	soda pop
bubble gum	food	computer	shelter
clothing	television	play	video game
necklace	safety	football	sleep
love	scooter	exercise	flowers

Follow Me

Speaking up is a healthy way to love ourselves and others. It helps us remember God's goodness inside. And it helps us make faithful choices.

Do speak up in situations like these three. *Draw a line from the beginning of each sentence to its correct ending. Then add what you would choose.*

1. You are in a restaurant. You are looking at the menu. Your tummy rumbles.

> I feel...   to have a treat.
> I think...   healthy food.
> I want...   hungry.
> I need...   that everything looks good.

What will you choose to eat? _____

_____

2. You are in class. Your teacher assigns a worksheet. You cannot concentrate on your work.

> I think...   confused.
> I feel...   that this worksheet is hard.
> I want...   help.
> I need...   the class to end.

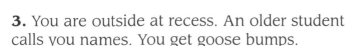

What will you choose to say and/or do? _____

_____

3. You are outside at recess. An older student calls you names. You get goose bumps.

> I think...   safety.
> I feel...   to stop the name-calling.
> I want...   that I might get hurt.
> I need...   afraid.

What will you choose to say and/or do? _____

_____

Come,

Here are...Five Ways to Pray

(See Luke 11:9, 13.)

Jesus encouraged his disciples to pray. He said,

> Ask and you will receive, search and you will find, knock and the door will be opened for you. God is ready to give the Holy Spirit to anyone who asks.

Prayer is talking and listening to God. There are many ways to pray—with thoughts, words, and actions, of course.

Recite prayers that you read from books and cards. Memorize some, too. Check off the ones you know:
___ Sign of the Cross ___Lord's Prayer ___Hail Mary
___Prayer of Praise ___Act of Contrition

Receive God's blessings. Have you ever noticed a bright rainbow? An ocean breeze? A friendly smile? Simply enjoy them!

Respond with thanks for blessings. Give thanks for problems, too. They can help you grow strong inside! Praise God with words like "Amen!" or "Awesome!"

Request God's help. Say what you think and feel. Say what you want and need. Sometimes it helps just to say it. God hears you!

Reflect on a choice you have made. Ask God to celebrate with you. Or ask God to forgive you. Then imagine a new choice for next time.

Prayerful choices are faithful choices!

Follow Me

Here are some prayers to **Read, Remember, and Recite**.

The Lord's Prayer

Our Father, who art in heaven,
hallowed be thy name;
thy kingdom come;
thy will be done on earth as it is in heaven.
Give us this day our daily bread;
and forgive us our trespasses
as we forgive those who trespass against us;
and lead us not into temptation,
but deliver us from evil. Amen.

The Hail Mary

Hail Mary, full of grace!
The Lord is with you!
Blessed are you
among women,
and blessed is the fruit
of your womb, Jesus.
Holy Mary, Mother of God,
pray for us sinners,
now and at the hour
of our death. Amen.

Prayer of Praise

Glory to the Father,
and to the Son,
and to the Holy Spirit.
As it was in the beginning,
is now,
and ever shall be. Amen.

Act of Contrition

My God,
I am sorry for my sins with all my heart.
In choosing to do wrong and in failing to do good,
I have sinned against you,
whom I should love above all things.
I firmly intend, with your help,
to do penance, to sin no more,
and to avoid whatever leads me to sin.
Our Savior Jesus Christ suffered and died for us.
In his name, my God, have mercy. Amen.

Come,

Receive God's blessings. They help us live and learn and love. Our senses help us notice them and enjoy them. How many blessings can you name? Start by filling in this chart.

See	rainbow		
Hear		bird	
Smell	rose		
Taste		apple	
Touch			hug

Respond with gratitude. Write "TYG" next to each blessing above. This means "Thank You, God." Keep noticing God's blessings. Try to name two each day. Write them on the calendar you will make below. Don't forget the "TYG"!

Request God's help for all your concerns. Make a prayer calendar for this month. Leave space to write on each date.

SUN	MON	TUE	WED	THU	FRI	SAT
				1	2	3
4	5	6	7	8	9	10
11	12	13	14	15	16	17
18	19	20	21	22	23	24
25	26	27	28	29	30	

14	15
John— Happy Birthday	Grandma— successful surgery

In the date's space, write your first name or the person you are praying for. Then add your request.

Keep the calendar where your family will see it. Leave a pencil with it, too. Ask everyone to add requests. Use the calendar when you pray alone or together. Is it helpful? If yes, make a new calendar for each new month!

Follow Me

Reflect on your choices.

*Start at **Number 1** and connect the dots. Stop at the green numbers and think about each statement. In your prayer, fill in the blanks.*

I am sorry about

_____.

5 ●

Today, I made
these choices

_____

_____.

3 ●

Tomorrow, I will

_____

_____.

● 7

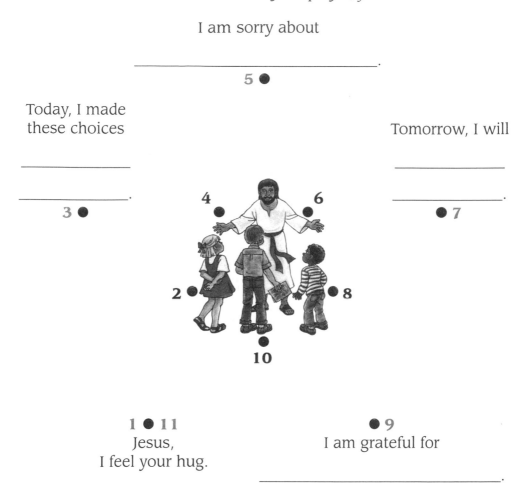

4 ●   6 ●

2 ●   ● 8

● 10

1 ● 11
Jesus,
I feel your hug.

● 9
I am grateful for

_____.

What happens each night? The stars come out to reflect their light. Use this prayer "**STAR**ter" each night before bed. Retrace the lines with your finger. Reflect on your choices from the day.

What happens each day? The sun comes up, hooray! Do your best to make faithful choices. That is how the Son shines through you!

Come,

Here are...Six Words to Remember

(See Matthew 6:12-14.)

Jesus taught his disciples about forgiveness. He said to pray with these words:

> Forgive us for doing wrong, as we forgive others.

Then Jesus explained.

> If you forgive others for the wrongs they do to you, your Father in heaven will forgive you, too.

God's mercy is bigger than we can imagine! The more we receive, the more we can share. The more we share, the more we can receive.

Everyone makes choices. Our choices affect other people. And their choices affect us, too. Some are helpful. Some are hurtful. Some are simply mistakes!

Sometimes people tell us when our choices are helpful or hurtful. Sometimes we just know. Something inside of us tells us. That "something" is our conscience.

Our conscience helps us know right from wrong. It is a signal from God's goodness deep inside. We "hear" it when we reflect on our choices. It is the Holy Spirit helping us.

When your choices are hurtful to someone else, remember these words:

I AM SORRY.

When someone's choices are hurtful to you, remember these words:

I FORGIVE YOU.

Follow Me

Reconciliation in Action

Decide which word goes in each sentence. Then write the word in the puzzle grid according to its sentence number.

1. God forgives us. We can _____ one another, too.
2. After a conflict, let your _____ settle down.
3. Imagine that Jesus is _____ beside you.
4. Jesus loves you very much. He _____ the other person, too.
5. Remember, God's _____ is inside both of you.
6. Say a _____. Ask the Holy Spirit to help you.
7. Now, make _____. Talk to the other person.
8. Be _____. Say "I am sorry" or "I forgive you."
9. Then _____ to what the other person says.
10. Take responsibility. Should you _____ something?

Word List

amends
close
feelings
forgive
goodness
honest
listen
loves
prayer
restore

These are all faithful choices. Here is one more.
Celebrate the Sacrament of Reconciliation!

Come,

Here are...Seven Works of Mercy

(See Matthew 25:37-40.)

Jesus promised to come back some day. He told a story about what will happen. He described what people will do. He said,

> Some people will ask, "When did we give you something to eat or drink? When did we welcome you as a stranger or give you clothes to wear or visit you while you were sick or in jail?"

And Jesus will answer them,

> Whenever you did it for any of my people, no matter how unimportant they seemed, you did it for me.

We don't know when Jesus will come back. But we do know what he wants! He wants us to help people with basic needs. And he doesn't want us to ignore them. Everyone is important!

When we help people with basic needs, we help Jesus with his mission. We bring more love into the world. Here are some ways to help people. Our Church calls them the "Corporal Works of Mercy." (*Corporal* means "of the body." So, the Corporal Works of Mercy feed and protect people's bodies.)

- **Feed the hungry.**
- **Give drink to the thirsty.**
- **Clothe the naked.**
- **Shelter the homeless.**
- **Visit the sick.**
- **Visit the imprisoned.**
- **Bury the dead.**

Whenever we do these things, we are making faithful choices. Some churches and schools collect groceries for food shelves, clothing for shelters, or books and greeting cards for people in hospitals or prisons. How about yours? How can you participate?

Follow Me

Color this stained-glass window. The pictures go with Jesus' story about helping others. In the lower right corner, draw yourself in as you did on page 5.

Now you are part of the story, too!
How can you share with people in need?

Come,

Here are...Eight Beautiful Attitudes
(See Matthew 5:1-10.)

Crowds of people followed Jesus. One day, he went up the side of a mountain. He gathered his disciples around him. Then he began to teach them. The crowds could hear him too. He said,

God blesses those people who depend only on God.
> They belong to the kingdom of heaven!

God blesses those people who grieve.
> They will find comfort!

God blesses those people who are humble.
> The earth will belong to them!

God blesses those people who long for fairness and work toward justice.
> They will be given what they want!

God blesses those people who are merciful.
> They will be treated with mercy!

God blesses those people whose hearts are pure.
> They will see God!

God blesses those people who make peace.
> They will be called God's children!

God blesses those people who are treated badly for doing the right things.
> They belong to the kingdom of heaven!

Attitudes are ways of thinking. They affect our choices. These beautiful attitudes are called "Beatitudes." They help us think like Jesus. They help us make faithful choices, too.

Follow Me

Here's some "food for thought" to help explain the Beatitudes. *Read each Beatitude on page 24. Then read its partner on the right. Find an ingredient to match, and fill in the blank.*

Ingredient List: "cheery-o" cereal, chocolate chips, mini marshmallows, oyster crackers, peanuts, popcorn, pretzels, raisins

1. We depend on God. The rain plumps us up and the sun dries us out. Now we are sweeter than ever! _____

2. We are salty, like tears of sadness. But we "stick" with God, who will "knot" abandon us! _____

3. We are what we are—nothing more, nothing less; not too bland, not too grand. We are a simple food, yet we "crack" people up sometimes. _____ _____

4. We work on being "hole-y" by being fair and just to others. Even our shape reminds us to "O"bey God. _____

_____

5. We are soft and sweet, even "mushy" on the inside. But we do not overpower any other flavors. _____ _____

6. We are honest from the inside out. We don't hide behind artificial flavors or colors. _____ _____

7. We are very close to our neighbors. We cooperate peacefully or we'll drive one another nuts! _____

8. We receive harsh treatment, but we totally trust God. After "taking the heat," we are transformed. _____

Now put 1 cup of each ingredient into a big bowl. Mix well. Enjoy this trail mix as you ponder the Beatitudes.

**You are on a journey of faith.
Follow Jesus with faithful choices!**

Come,

Here are...Nine Fruits of the Spirit

(See Luke 8:4-15.)

Jesus taught lessons by telling stories. In one story, Jesus told about a farmer who scattered seeds. They fell on all kinds of soil. Jesus explained what he meant. He said,

> The seed is God's message. Those seeds that fell on good ground are the people who listen to the message and keep it in good and honest hearts.
> They last and produce a harvest.

It takes a long time for a seed to grow, mature, and produce fruit. Our faith is like that, too.

We receive God's message through Jesus and our Church community. We keep God's message in good and honest hearts. And we do our best to make faithful choices. That is how we grow in faith.

The Holy Spirit helps us. How do we know?
We produce this harvest:

(See directions on page 27.)

1. _____

2. _____

3. _____

4. _____

5. _____

6. _____

7. _____

8. _____

9. _____

(See Galatians 5:22-23.)

Follow Me

The **Fruits of the Spirit** ripen as we grow in faith.

Follow the lines below to discover their names. Write the words on page 26.

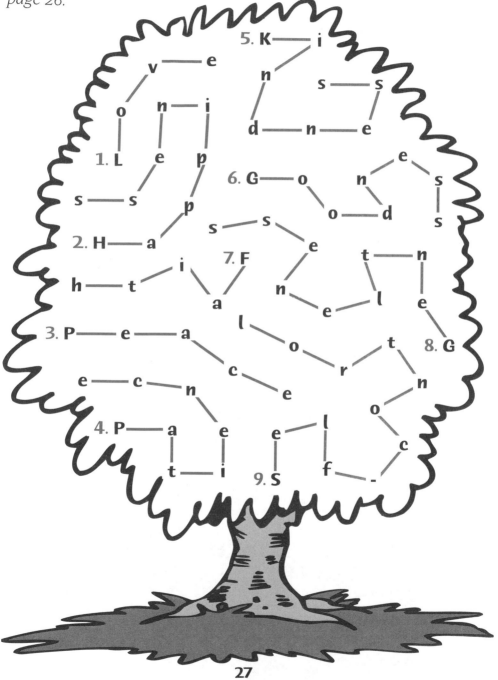

Come,
Here are... Ten Commandments

Jesus said,

> I did not come to do away with the Laws, but to give them their full meaning.
>
> (Matthew 5:17)

What are the commandments and what do they mean? *Block out every J and Z in the tablets on this page and the next. Read the remaining the words.*

```
          J Z J Z J Z
       Z J Z J Z J Z J Z J
     J Z J Z  THE  TEN  J Z J Z
   Z J Z  COMMANDMENTS  J Z J
 J Z J Z J Z J Z J Z J Z J Z J Z J Z J Z J
Z J Z J Z J Z J Z J Z J Z J Z J Z J Z J Z J
J Z J Z 1 Z I Z A M J Y O U R Z G O D Z J J Z J Z
Z H A V E Z N O J G O D S Z B E S I D E S Z M E
J Z P U T J Y O U R Z T R U S T Z I N J M E Z J
Z J Z J Z J Z J Z J Z J Z J Z J Z J Z J Z J Z J
J Z J Z J Z J Z J Z J Z J Z J Z J Z J Z J Z J Z
Z J Z 2 Z R E S P E C T Z M Y J N A M E Z J Z J
S P E A K Z O F J M E Z I N J H O L Y Z W A Y S
Z D O J N O T J S W E A R J A B O U T J M E Z J
J Z J Z J Z J Z J Z J Z J Z J Z J Z J Z J Z J Z
Z J Z J Z J Z J Z J Z J Z J Z J Z J Z J Z J Z J
J 3 J H O N O R J T H E Z S A B B A T H J Z J Z
Z J Z T A K E J T I M E Z T O J P R A Y Z J Z J
J Z J Z T A K E J T I M E Z T O J P L A Y Z J Z
Z T A K E J A J B R E A K J F R O M Z W O R K J
J Z T A K E J T I M E Z F O R Z F A M I L Y J Z
Z J Z J Z J Z J Z J Z J Z J Z J Z J Z J Z J Z J
```

Follow Me

Jesus said,

If you obey [the Laws] and teach others its commands, you will have an important place in the kingdom.

(Matthew 5:19)

The **Ten Commandments** tell us about God's loving plan for us. *Look on page 6. Decide which of the two Greatest Commandments fits each tablet. Write it sideways next to the tablet.*

```
        Z J Z J Z J
      J Z J Z J Z J Z J Z J Z
    Z J Z J Z J Z J Z J Z J Z J Z
   4 Z H O N O R Z Y O U R J P A R E N T S
  Z L I S T E N J A N D J C O O P E R A T E J Z
 J Z J Z J Z J Z J Z J Z J Z J Z J Z J Z J Z J Z
 Z J Z J Z 5 Z D O J N O T J K I L L Z J Z J Z J
 J Z J Z R E S P E C T Z A L L Z L I F E J Z J Z
 Z T A K E J C A R E Z O F J T H E J E A R T H J
 J Z J Z J Z J Z J Z J Z J Z J Z J Z J Z J Z J Z
 Z 6 Z R E S P E C T Z E V E R Y Z B O D Y J Z J
 B E J L O Y A L J T O Z Y O U R J F R I E N D S
 J Z J Z J Z J Z J Z J Z J Z J Z J Z J Z J Z J Z
 Z J Z J Z 7 Z D O J N O T J S T E A L J Z J Z J
 J Z B E J F A I R Z T O J E A C H Z O T H E R Z
 Z J Z J Z J Z J Z J Z J Z J Z J Z J Z J Z J Z J
 J Z J Z 8 Z T E L L J T H E J T R U T H J Z J Z
 Z J Z J Z J Z J Z J Z J Z J Z J Z J Z J Z J Z J
 J Z 9 Z R E S P E C T Z A L L Z P E O P L E J Z
 Z J Z J Z J Z J Z J Z J Z J Z J Z J Z J Z J Z J
 1 0 J R E S P E C T J A L L J P R O P E R T Y Z
 J Z J Z J Z J Z J Z J Z J Z J Z J Z J Z J Z J Z
```

The Ten Commandments bring us back to the basics. Jesus brings us beyond! He fulfills God's promise to all of us.

Use this picture code to find the words of that promise.

Code

=A	=E	=I	=O	=T
=B	=F	=L	=P	=U
=C	=G	=M	=R	=W
=D	=H	=N	=S	=Y

I WILL WRITE MY

LAWS ON THEIR

HEART AND MINDS.

I WILL BE THEIR

GOD AND THEY WILL

BE MY PEOPLE. (Jeremiah 31:33)

As we follow Jesus, we become more and more like him—from the inside out! Then we follow the commandments because our own hearts tell us to. That is God's grace-filled promise. That is what true freedom is all about.

Here is...A Review

You are learning a lot about making choices!

Count on Jesus. Keep following him. And keep making faithful choices! Sometimes they will be difficult or unpopular or even boring. But don't give up. God will bless you in BIG ways. God's ways are bigger and deeper than you can imagine!

Count on parents and teachers to help you. Count on friends, too. Faithful choices are easier when you help one another.

Count on this book, too. Review it often. It will remind you of many faithful choices. Here is the countdown!

Ten . . . Commandments
Nine . . . Fruits of the Spirit
Eight . . . Beautiful Attitudes
Seven . . . Works of Mercy
Six . . . . . Words to Remember
Five . . . . Ways to Pray
Four . . . . Ways to Speak Up
Three . . . Ways to Love One Another
Two . . . . Greatest Commandments

What about **One**? Use the picture code on the opposite page to find out what completes this countdown. It is:

Answers

1. Look up to love God above us.
2. Reach out to love people among us.
Eight extra words: share, mind, thank, soul, care, strength, praise, heart

Page 9
God made us equally. Do not look down on anyone. Look for goodness in everyone.

Page 10
1. please, thank you 2. hello, goodbye
3. excuse me 4. yes please; no thank you
5. STOP, HELP

Page 13

Page 14
Needs: air, water, food, shelter, clothing, play, safety, sleep, love, exercise
Wants: candy, soda pop, bubble gum, computer, television, video game, necklace, football, scooter, flowers

Page 15
1. I feel...hungry. I think...that everything looks good. I want...to have a treat. I need...healthy food.
2. I think...that this worksheet is hard. I feel...confused. I want...the class to end. I need...help.
3. I think...that I might get hurt. I feel... afraid. I want...to stop the name-calling. I need...safety.

Page 21
1. forgive; 2. feelings; 3. close; 4. loves;
5. goodness; 6. prayer; 7. amends;
8. honest; 9. listen; 10. restore

Page 25
1. raisins; 2. pretzels; 3. oyster crackers;
4. "cheery o" cereal; 5. mini marshmallows;
6. chocolate chips; 7. peanuts; 8. popcorn

Pages 26-27
1. love; 2. happiness; 3. peace; 4. patience;
5. kindness; 6. goodness; 7. faith;
8. gentleness; 9. self-control

Pages 28-29
Left tablet: Love God.
Right tablet: Love others.
(All other answers are self-revealing.)

Page 30
I will write my laws on their hearts and minds. I will be their God and they will be my people.

Page 31
One incredible faithful you!